Scribble Scrabble Writing Journal For Kids

By Beatrice M. Young

©2009 Beatrice M. Young

Published by

Etosha **P**ublications
www.etoshapublications.com

This book is dedicated to God for giving me the gift to write,
To my mother, Rita M. Clay for inspiring me to write,
To the love of my life, Simba and my precious jewels, Ebony, Tasha,
Harmonie and Per'Shawn for believing in me as a writer,
And to my family and friends for their encouragement and faith in me.

Animal Antics

If you could be any animal in the world, describe what kind of animal you would be. Why did you choose to be this animal? Think about it!

Write about it!

Scribble Scrabble Writing Journal for Kids

Scribble Scrabble Writing Journal for Kids

Memories of My Favorite Things

Close your eyes for a moment and think about the most exciting thing you ever saw. Think hard. What was it? How did you feel when you saw it? Write down whatever you can remember. Think about it!

Write about it!

_____
_____
_____
_____
_____
_____
_____
_____
_____
_____
_____

Scribble Scrabble Writing Journal for Kids

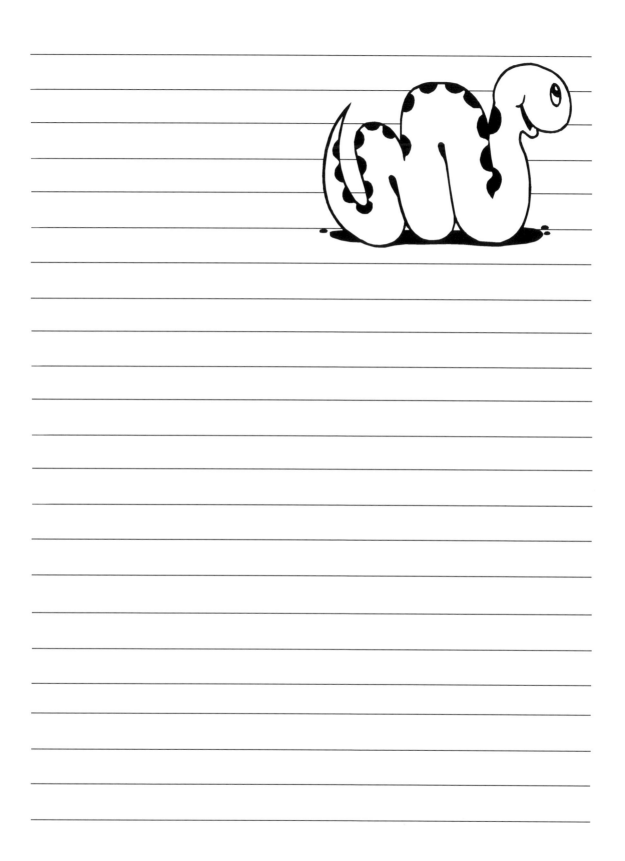

Scribble Scrabble Writing Journal for Kids

My Planet

Pretend you are from another planet far beyond the galaxy. Describe everything about your planet. Think about it!

Write about it!

_____
_____
_____
_____
_____
_____
_____
_____
_____
_____

Scribble Scrabble Writing Journal for Kids

Scribble Scrabble Writing Journal for Kids

It's A Perfect Day

What is a perfect day? Imagine what a perfect day would be like and write it down. How would you feel on the perfect day? Think about it!

Write about it!

Scribble Scrabble Writing Journal for Kids

Scribble Scrabble Writing Journal for Kids

The Greatest Invention in the World

You are an inventor and you just created the greatest invention in the world! Describe your new invention. How will your invention help others. You can draw pictures of it if you'd like. Think about it!

Write about it!

_____
_____
_____
_____
_____
_____
_____
_____
_____
_____
_____

Scribble Scrabble Writing Journal for Kids

Scribble Scrabble Writing Journal for Kids

Invention for Sale!

Now, let's sell your invention! Tell people all about your invention and how to buy it. You can draw pictures if you'd like. Think about it!

Write about it!

_____
_____
_____
_____
_____
_____
_____
_____
_____
_____

Scribble Scrabble Writing Journal for Kids

SALE

Scribble Scrabble Writing Journal for Kids

How Do I get to Your House?

How far is your school from your house? Describe how to get to your house from school. If you don't know, just make it up. Draw a map if you'd like. Think about it!

Write about it!

_____
_____
_____
_____
_____
_____
_____
_____
_____

Scribble Scrabble Writing Journal for Kids

Scribble Scrabble Writing Journal for Kids

Where Did the Dinosaurs Go?

What do YOU think REALLY happened the day the dinosaurs disappeared? Where did the dinosaurs go? Think about it!

Write about it!

_____
_____
_____
_____
_____
_____
_____
_____
_____
_____
_____
_____

Scribble Scrabble Writing Journal for Kids

Scribble Scrabble Writing Journal for Kids

If I Were A Superhero

Who is your favorite superhero? If you were a superhero, what would you do? Think about it!

Write about it!

_____
_____
_____
_____
_____
_____
_____
_____
_____
_____

Scribble Scrabble Writing Journal for Kids

Scribble Scrabble Writing Journal for Kids

Meet the Press

Interview someone you want to learn more about. Ask the person to tell you about something special that happened to them, then write a newspaper article about it. Think about it!

Write about it!

_____
_____
_____
_____
_____
_____
_____
_____
_____
_____

Scribble Scrabble Writing Journal for Kids

Scribble Scrabble Writing Journal for Kids

Eyes Like Stars

Do you know what a simile is? A simile is a word or group of words that compare one thing to something different like "hungry as a horse" or "slow as molasses." Write a short story about your favorite thing to do and add a simile or two, or three, or as many as you would like. Think about it!

Write about it!

Scribble Scrabble Writing Journal for Kids

Scribble Scrabble Writing Journal for Kids

The Moral of the Story

Write a story to teach a four year old why they should or should not do something. What kind of story do you want to tell? Think about it!

Write about it!

_____
_____
_____
_____
_____
_____
_____
_____
_____
_____
_____

Scribble Scrabble Writing Journal for Kids

Scribble Scrabble Writing Journal for Kids

What Would Baby Bear Say?

Have you ever read Goldie Locks and the Three Bears? How would Baby Bear tell the story? What would a bird in a tree say happened? What do YOU think really happened to Goldie Locks and the Three Bears? Think about it!

Write about it!

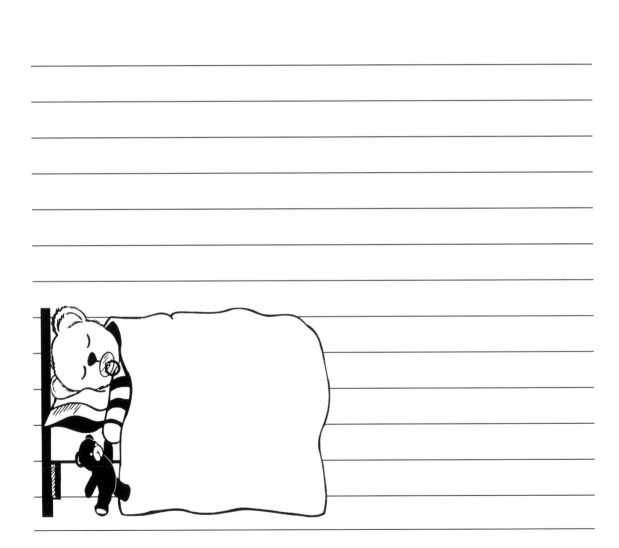

Scribble Scrabble Writing Journal for Kids

Scribble Scrabble Writing Journal for Kids

King and Queen for a Day

If you were voted king or queen for a day, what would you do? Think about it!

Write about it!

Scribble Scrabble Writing Journal for Kids

Scribble Scrabble Writing Journal for Kids

Raging Red

Close your eyes and think of a color. Describe the color you saw. Was it your favorite color or did you create a new one? What does the color mean to you? Think about it!

Write about it!

Scribble Scrabble Writing Journal for Kids

Scribble Scrabble Writing Journal for Kids

Music to My Ears

Close your eyes and listen to some music. How does the music make you feel? What do you do when you hear the music? Think about it!

Write about it!

_____
_____
_____
_____
_____
_____
_____
_____
_____
_____
_____
_____

Scribble Scrabble Writing Journal for Kids

Scribble Scrabble Writing Journal for Kids

There's a Fish in My Living Room

Have you ever seen a fish sit on a couch and watch TV? Have you ever seen a pig fly or mice dance on the moon? Write a funny story where everything in the world is wacky. Think about it!

Write about it!

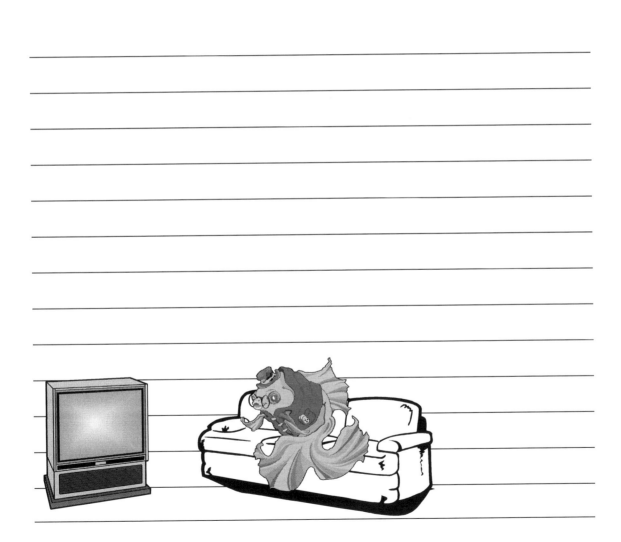

Scribble Scrabble Writing Journal for Kids

Scribble Scrabble Writing Journal for Kids

What Do You Want to Do When You Grow Up?

What do you want to DO when you grow up? What do you like best about your work? Think about it!

Write about it!

Scribble Scrabble Writing Journal for Kids

Scribble Scrabble Writing Journal for Kids

The Greatest Adventure in the World

What is your greatest adventure in the world? Where do you go? What do you do? Think about it!

Write about it!

_____
_____
_____
_____
_____
_____
_____
_____
_____
_____
_____

Scribble Scrabble Writing Journal for Kids

Scribble Scrabble Writing Journal for Kids

Freestyle!

Freestyle is like recess at school. You can write about anything you want! Whatever you think, whatever you feel...

Write about it!

_____
_____
_____
_____
_____
_____
_____
_____
_____
_____

Scribble Scrabble Writing Journal for Kids

Scribble Scrabble Writing Journal for Kids

Made in the USA
Lexington, KY
23 March 2014